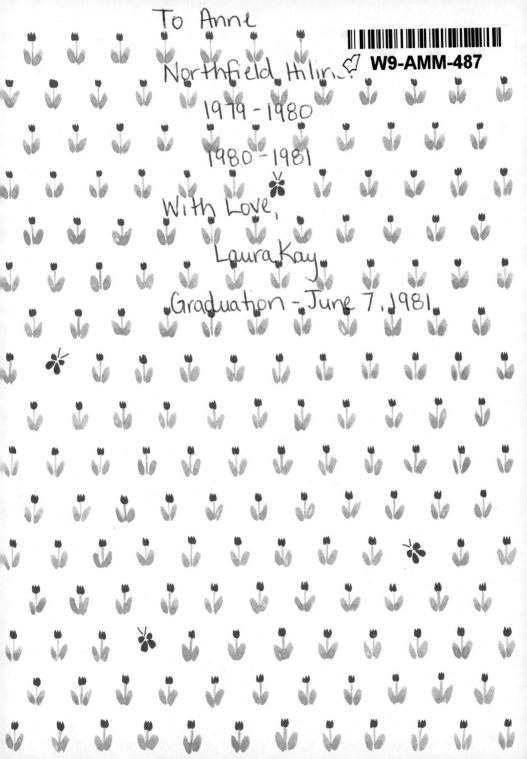

To Anne

Northfield Hiline

1979-1980

1980-1981

With Love,

Laura Kay

Graduation - June 7, 1981

To Every Thing There Is A Season

To Every Thing There Is A Season

Writings That Celebrate Life's Many Joys

Selected by Stephanie C. Oda

Designed and illustrated
by Bonnie Weber

The C. R. Gibson Company
Norwalk, Connecticut

And He saw every thing that He had made, and, behold, it was very good.

To every thing there is a season, and a time to every purpose under the heaven:
A time to be born, and a time to die; a time to plant, and a time to pluck up that which is planted;
A time to kill, and a time to heal; a time to break down, and a time to build up;
A time to weep, and a time to laugh; a time to mourn, and a time to dance;
A time to cast away stones, and a time to gather stones together; a time to embrace, and a time to refrain from embracing;
A time to get, and a time to lose; a time to keep, and a time to cast away;
A time to rend, and a time to sew; a time to keep silence, and a time to speak;
A time to love, and a time to hate; a time of war, and a time of peace.

Eccles. 3:1-8

A MORNING WISH

The sun is just rising on the morning of another day. What can I wish that this day may bring me? Nothing that shall make the world or others poorer, nothing at the expense of other men; but just those few things which in their coming do not stop with me but touch me rather, as they pass and gather strength.

A few friends, who understand me, and yet remain my friends.

A work to do which has real value, without which the world would feel the poorer.

A return for such work small enough not to tax anyone who pays.

A mind unafraid to travel, even though the trail be not blazed.

An understanding heart.

A sight of the eternal hills, and the unresting sea, and of something beautiful which the hand of man has made.

A sense of humor, and the power to laugh. A little leisure with nothing to do.

A few moments of quiet, silent meditation. The sense of the presence of God.

And the patience to wait for the coming of these things, with the wisdom to know them when they come, and the wit not to change this morning wish of mine.

Walter Reid Hunt

I am at one with everything, O Universe, which is
      well-fitting in thee.
Nothing to me is early or late which is timely with thee.
All is fruit to me that thy seasons bring.
O Nature, from thee are all things, in thee are all things,
      to thee all things return . . .

Marcus Aurelius

SPRING THUNDER

Listen. The wind is still,
And far away in the night—
See! The uplands fill
With a running light.

Open the doors. It is warm;
And where the sky was clear—
Look! The head of a storm
That marches here!

Come under the trembling hedge—
Fast, although you fumble.
There! Did you hear the edge
Of winter crumble?

Mark Van Doren

THE PROMISE OF SPRING

Now is that strange hushed time of year when Nature seems to pause. The winds of winter are wearied. The weeds, once ranked high in the fields, are low and subject. The weathered leaves begin to fall from the oaks that have clutched them fiercely, as the old clutch at little comforts.

The moment is like a pause in a symphony, when the great composer brings the fury of his music to a stop, a rest so fateful and significant that in the silence the listener counts his own loud heartbeats as though they were his last—hoping for and almost dreading the beginning of the new theme in the next measures.

And what will it be, that melody, but the beginning of spring? The talk of thaw in many runnels, the sounds of birds finding again their voices, of tree toads trilling in chill twilights, of a spade that strikes a stone.

Donald Culross Peattie

For, lo, the winter is past, the rain is over and gone; The flowers appear on the earth; the time of the singing of birds is come, and the voice of the turtle is heard in our land.

Song of Sol. 2:11, 12

A glimpse of the outside world on an early spring day moved Anne Frank to write these words in her beloved diary—words that express hope, courage and an irrepressible joy of spirit.

Wednesday, 23 February, 1944

It's lovely weather outside and I've quite perked up since yesterday. Nearly every morning I go to the attic where Peter works to blow the stuffy air out of my lungs. From my favorite spot on the floor I look up at the blue sky and the bare chestnut tree, on whose branches little raindrops shine, appearing like silver, and at the seagulls and other birds as they glide on the wind.

I looked out of the open window over a large area of Amsterdam, over all the roofs and on to the horizon, which was such a pale blue that it was hard to see the dividing line. "As long as this exists," I thought, "and I may live to see it, this sunshine, the cloudless skies, while this lasts, I cannot be unhappy."

The best remedy for those who are afraid, lonely, or unhappy is to go outside, somewhere where they can be quite alone with the heavens, nature, and God. Because only then does one feel that all is as it should be and that God wishes to see people happy, amidst the simple beauty of nature. As long as this exists, and it certainly always will, I know that then there will always be comfort for every sorrow, whatever the circumstances may be.

Yours, Anne

ONLY THE EARTH ENDURES

Some things will never change. Some things will always be the same. Lean down your ear upon the earth, and listen.

The voice of forest water in the night, a woman's laughter in the dark, the clean, hard rattle of raked gravel, the cricketing stitch of midday in hot meadows, the delicate web of children's voices in bright air—these things will never change.

The glitter of sunlight on roughened water, the glory of the stars, the innocence of morning, the smell of the sea in harbors, the feathery blur and smoky buddings of young boughs, and something there that comes and goes and never can be captured, the thorn of spring, the sharp and tongueless cry—these things will always be the same.

All things belonging to the earth will never change—the leaf, the blade, the flower, the wind that cries and sleeps and wakes again, the trees whose stiff arms clash and tremble in the dark, and the dust of lovers long since buried in the earth—all things proceeding from the earth to seasons, all things that lapse and change and come again upon the earth—these things will always be the same, for they come up from the earth that never changes, they go back into the earth that lasts forever. Only the earth endures, but it endures forever.

The tarantula, the adder, and the asp will also never change. Pain and death will always be the same. But under the pavements trembling like a pulse, under the buildings trembling like a cry, under the waste of time, under the hoof of the beast above the broken bones of cities, there will be something growing like a flower, something bursting from the earth again, forever deathless, faithful, coming into life again like April.

Thomas Wolfe

While the earth remaineth, seedtime and harvest, and cold and heat, and summer and winter, and day and night shall not cease.

Gen. 8:22

All year round, whatever the season, there can be rebirth. Spring is but a symbol, and Easter commemorates the victory over death as spring marks the emergence from destructive winter. Every day, perhaps every minute, somewhere in the tired world a spirit is reborn.

Faith Baldwin

REBIRTH IN THE COUNTRY

I came here eight years ago as the renter of this farm, of which soon afterward I became the owner. The time before that I like to forget. The chief impression it left upon my memory, now happily growing indistinct, is of being hurried faster than I could well travel. From the moment, as a boy of seventeen, I first began to pay my own way, my days were ordered by an inscrutable power which drove me hourly to my task. . . .

For many years, and I can say it truthfully, I never rested. I neither thought nor reflected. I had no pleasure, even though I pursued it fiercely during the brief respite of vacations. Through many feverish years I did not work: I merely produced. . . .

All these things happened in cities and among crowds. I like to forget them. They smack of that slavery of the spirit which is so much worse than mere slavery of the body.

One day—it was in April, I remember, and the soft maples in the city park were just beginning to blossom—I stopped suddenly. I did not intend to stop. I confess in humiliation that it was no courage, no will of my own. I intended to go on toward Success: but Fate stopped me. . . . I lay prostrate with fever and close to death for weeks and watched the world go by. . . .

And thus, eight years ago, I came here like one sore-wounded creeping from the field of battle. . . .

For a time in the new life, I was happy to drunkenness—working, eating, sleeping. I was an animal again, let out to run in green pastures. I was glad of the sunrise and the sunset. I was glad at noon. It delighted me when my muscles ached with work and when, after supper, I could not keep my eyes open for sheer weariness. And sometimes I was awakened in the night

out of a sound sleep—seemingly by the very silences—
and lay in a sort of bodily comfort impossible to describe.

I did not want to feel or think: I merely wanted to
live. In the sun or the rain I wanted to go out and come
in, and never again to know the pain of the unquiet
spirit. . . .

But like all birth, it came, at last, suddenly. . . . I was
plowing in my upperfield—not then mine in fact—and it
was a soft afternoon with the earth turning up moist and
fragrant. . . .

I stopped there in the field and looked up. And it was
as if I had never looked up before. I discovered another
world. I had been there before, for long and long, but I
had never seen nor felt it. All discoveries are made in that
way: a man finds a new thing, not in nature but in
himself.

It was as though, concerned with plow and harness
and furrow I had never known that the world had height
or color or sweet sounds, or that there was *feeling* in a
hillside. I forgot myself, or where I was. I stood a long
time motionless. My dominant feeling, if I can at all
express it, was of a strange new friendliness, a warmth,
as though these hills, this field about me, the woods, had
suddenly spoken to me and caressed me. It was as
though I had been accepted in membership, as though I
was now recognized, after long trial, as belonging here.

David Grayson

A great musician one day visited the celebrated painter Matisse at his home on the shores of the Mediterranean. He asked Matisse, "What is your inspiration?"

"I grow artichokes," replied Matisse. "Every morning I go into the garden and watch these plants. I see the play of light and shade on the leaves and I discover new combinations of colors and fantastic patterns. They inspire me. Then I go back into the studio and paint."

John H. Crowe

Growth is the only evidence of life.

John Henry, Cardinal Newman

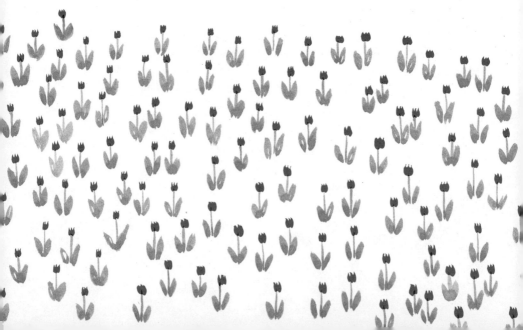

AT DAWN

If every day is a repetition of life, every dawn signs as it were a new contract with existence. At dawn everything is fresh, light, simple, as it is for children. At dawn spiritual truth, like the atmosphere, is more transparent, and our organs, like the young leaves, drink in the light more eagerly, breathe in more ether, and less of things earthly. If night and the starry sky speak to the meditative soul of God, of eternity and the infinite, the dawn is the time for projects, for resolutions, for the birth of action. While the silence and the 'sad serenity of the azure vault' incline the soul to self-recollection, the vigour and gaiety of nature spread into the heart and make it eager for life and living.—Spring is upon us. Primroses and violets have already hailed her coming. Rash blooms are showing on the peach trees; the swollen buds of the pear trees and the lilacs point to the blossoming that is to be; the honeysuckles are already green.

Amiel

Everything that is done in the world is done by hope.

Martin Luther

THE MIRACLE OF EASTER

The idea of resurrection is a most fascinating one. I am glad that Christ's resurrection came in spring. It couldn't have happened in a more likely month than April, judging from the part of the earth where I was born and grew to manhood. I do not know about the Holy Land, where Christ was born, lived, and was crucified, whether there are four distinct seasons or not. I doubt it. I have been in Istanbul, Turkey, which is not a great distance away, and they do not have our four distinct seasons there. Yet this spring month of April is beautiful in almost every part of the world.

Since I have grown up in this valley on little farms, helped my father plow the creek bottoms and the steep slopes on the hillside, hoe the plants, and later harvest the crops in autumn, I cannot doubt resurrection. How can any farmer ever doubt resurrection? Though there have been periods that I didn't go to church, often when I was away a year or more at a time, there was never a time when I doubted the resurrection of Christ. He was the seed of God planted in the earth, the Son of God sent to show us the way. Only after death, the kind of death we know, He was called by God and came from the tomb and ascended into Heaven. It is a beautiful idea.

The man who has never planted a seed in the ground would be the first to doubt the story of the resurrection. One of the first things we have always planted in the spring has been our Irish potatoes. We plant them on Good Friday, the day of Christ's crucifixion. I have seen snow fall on our potatoes and the ground get cold. I have seen it freeze. The potatoes would lie lifeless in the cold ground. Then suddenly the crumpled dark-green leaves would peep up through the rough dark crust of earth. The potato seed had resurrected. And through the spring and early summer we hoed these potatoes and kept the weeds cut down. In autumn, after their summer's growing season was over and their vines had withered, we dug our potatoes. We put them in the cellar and the next spring planted from our own seed. Here was the process of eternal life—growing, living, dying, and rebirth.

Jesse Stuart

GARDENING

Until the future blossoms on your limbs
And the sap blooms that pushes through your veins,
Taking its time among your growing pains,
You order in their vase chrysanthemums
Or whatever bud offers you its stem
This bursting season. Taken from the rain
The petals spread, flashing their color, wane,
Then drop upon the polished floor, like crumbs.

Before your breaking forth, I see you touch
The fallen petals, wondering if you hear
Your sighs, like shears, clipping the heart of me,
Wondering if, grown up, you'll know how much
One's blood can tremble when a child who's dear
Goes to her knees beside the flowering tree.

Dabney Stuart

If you don't overcome self-pity, the game's all over. My father taught us there was no time for self-pity in life. You had work to do. On the plains of South Dakota, adversity was part of daily life. I remember the dust storms, the blizzards, the summer heat and droughts. Yet when the crops failed, you always thought, *There's another year coming. I'll prepare the soil and pray.* You were always future-oriented.

Hubert Humphrey

LET ME GROW

I faced another birthday last week, Lord. They seem to be getting closer and closer together. And upon looking in the mirror I observed that this past year had left traces of its pressures in visible signs of destruction.

If those crow's-feet at the corners of the eyes are in reality laugh lines, I must have spent a hilarious year. And if that sprinkling of fine white hairs insinuating themselves among the fall of brown proclaims maturity— Lord, I have come of age.

I used to think my parents were old when they were thirty-five. And when they celebrated their twenty-fifth wedding anniversary, I thought they were ancient! But now I find that with each year comes a new kind of youth. Life is so full of surprises; it's good to be alive.

Let me grow young as I grow old, Lord. But most of all, let me grow.

Jean Reynolds Davis

CONTENTMENT

When spring arrives and lilacs blow
I'm not compelled to shovel snow.
In summer no one bothers me
To feed the fire, nor skate, nor ski.
In autumn no one longer needs
To waste the morning pulling weeds.
And winter brings no dewy dawn
When I must rise to mow the lawn.

So I am glad the seasons through
For what I do not have to do.

Arthur Guiterman

THE SEASON MADE FOR JOYS

Youth's the season made for joys,
*   Love is then our duty:*
She alone who that employs
*   Well deserves her beauty.*
*   Let's be gay*
*   While we may:*
Beauty's a flower despised in decay.

Let us drink and sport today,
*   Ours is not tomorrow.*
Love with youth flies swift away:
*   Age is nought but sorrow.*
*   Dance and sing*
*   Time's on the wing:*
Life never knows the return of Spring.

John Gay

By walking, we see more of the world closest to us. We can look at a tree, or a flower, or talk to a neighbor. Walking slows us down and lets us take a closer look at life. Whether we walk to work—if we're fortunate enough to live that near our employment—or to church, or to the neighborhood grocery, we'll discover new insights into what makes our world beautiful. Indeed, an old-fashioned walk can be a marvelous tonic.

J. Spencer Kinard

Walking down a country lane, a man heard his little granddaughter from the other side of a large bush. She was repeating the alphabet—A, B, C, D, E, but in an oddly reverent sort of way. He waited until she was through and then walked around to find her.

"What were you doing?" he asked.

"I was praying," she answered. "I couldn't think of the right words, so I just said the letters, and God will put them together into the words, because He knows what I was thinking."

Robert E. Goodrich, Jr.

The glorious month of May—what better time to pay tribute to motherhood? Hal Boyle does it engagingly in an open letter to his mother.

Dear Mom,

You are one of the world's hardest gals to please on Mother's Day.

The ordinary presents are no good at all. You don't want jewelry. If your children buy you flowers or candy, you say, "It's just a waste of money." They can't give you money with any sense of satisfaction because they know you won't spend it on yourself. You'll just put it away in an old sock for your grandchildren.

"Oh, don't give me anything—Mother's Day is just a bunch of nonsense," you say. Your happiest Mother's Days have been the ones on which you spent five hours turning your face cherry red over a cookstove fixing a family feast—in the years when the whole family could be there to enjoy it.

What could one who was away do to please you except to call you long distance and tell you he missed you and wished he was home? It is hard to give anything to a woman who has spent her life in giving to others.

The only thing I have to offer you is the one thing you never asked for—appreciation.

Why do I love you? Let me count the reasons—just a few:

I love you because you are my mother, not only of my body but of my spirit's hunger.

I love you because when I deserved and needed a switching I got it—not later, but right then when I knew I had done wrong, felt guilty, and recognized I should be punished.

I love you because you never let tomorrow's sun rise on yesterday's anger.

I love you because you played no favorites among your children. Your only favorite child (this is still true) was the one that most needed your understanding help at the time.

I love you because when the cat had too many kittens you couldn't bear to have them drowned. (With five kids yourself you could understand the mother cat's problem.)

I love you because, although you had only a third-grade education, you never ceased reading and learning and widening the horizon of your own mind. And from your mind my mind caught fire.

I love you because you always watered and fed my adolescent dreams.

I love you because, when Dad died nearly 19 years ago, you refused to turn into a self-pitying widow. Time has mellowed you. It cannot shrivel or defeat you.

I love you because, now that your children have grown, you refuse to try to run their lives. You merely say mildly "learn to sit loosely in the saddle of life."

I love you because, although you and I have always felt free to talk to each other about anything, from the whims of God to the frailties of man, I feel I really know less about you than almost anyone I know at all. You have always held a mystery to me, you always will. The more you love people, the more you realize there is a part of them you cannot ever know.

Finally, I love you because I know that when you read this you will be embarrassed and say, "Now, why did he have to do that? Can't he think of something more important to write about than that?"

Well, not today, Mom.

Respectfully,
Your long son,
Harold

According to Mama, there is no problem that will not be a little bit solved by the coming of spring. I grew up believing that there was only one correct way to end a discussion of things unpleasant or troublesome: nod at the calendar, pat somebody on the back if possible, and sigh, "Maybe in the spring . . . "

Helene Melyan

She openeth her mouth with wisdom; and in her tongue is the law of kindness.
She looketh well to the ways of her household, and eateth not the bread of idleness.
Her children arise up, and call her blessed; her husband also, and he praiseth her.

Prov. 31:26-28

ISN'T MOM BEAUTIFUL

Kristy was in junior-high school. She came home one night after school to a big discovery. Her dad was sitting at the kitchen table having a beer. He'd been painting the house and now he was winding down another day's work. Kristy joined him with a Coke and they visited.

Through the window she caught a view of her mom on the ladder. Her folks were having a lot of fun painting the house. They had decided to do it this year on her dad's vacation. So there was Mom, carefully applying those last strokes on her section, and she was a sight. Old gray hat. Baggy pants. Shirttail hanging out and every bit of her thoroughly splattered.

Kristy and her dad had always conversed well. Nothing heavy now. Just fun talk. She chattered on about school, friends, plus miscellany. And all the while her dad kept glancing out the window. Suddenly, with a look she'd never recognized before, he said from deep inside, "Isn't Mom beautiful?"

Here's how Kristy now describes it.

"I couldn't tell you the number of times I've thought back to that day. How my dad looked, the tone of his voice, the depth of feeling. First time I'd ever noticed my mom as a female figure. Right then I knew she was very female, especially when she looked through the window and made a face.

"Anyway, I sensed something wonderful about my mom and dad I'd never felt before. It was a very special day in my life. One of those mystical moments for a girl growing up."

Dr. Charlie Shedd

WHEN SUMMER BURSTS

In the upward drift of spring, I accumulate a longing for the ultimate confrontation with blaze and brilliance—summer; the sun and the year at their zenith. Daily, as earth turns, a fragile thread of tension pulls ever more taut in me. I begin to ask: "Is it now?"

In our garden, bees thrum over a multitude of blossoms and spiral exultantly into the sky—but the sky is not yet the blue of summer. A baby, last year a-drowse with newness on his mother's shoulder, this year makes his first barefoot tracks in dew-tipped grass. Still, summer has not come—quite.

Girls in pretty dresses are faintly gilded; soft shadows shorten at noon; boys strip for a first swing off a rope into a country pond, and surface in a thrash of shivering surprise—how can water be so chill when the calendar now says summer? When, *when,* will the sun be hot enough to brown the girls, bedazzle every noontide, and warm the water for adventuring boys?

At last, on the fourth morning of July, the fine thread of tension snaps: a boy wakes, blinks happily at sight of a glory day, and at once reaches under his pillow for a fingerlength of forbidden firecracker. He lights it with a match and hurls it out his window. Thus summer begins with a bang; and from one end of the country to the other, 20 million kids are tossed from their beds by that joyful noise.

I wake and listen. With an inward thump of pleasure, I too salute the Fourth. "Hurrah for the splendid racket of liberty!" I think. "Hurrah for summer begun!"

For it is summer indeed. On this morning, who can doubt it? Lofty at the peak of poles, sun-bright, spangled banners lift on the shimmering air. Fresh breezes enter summer rooms and blow away a wintering of secret scents—mice, must, mothballs and memories. The ocean glints silvery and restless, sifting pebbles, patterning the sand. In clear lakes, fish sink into cooler waters, while just-christened motorboats putt past above. Today the grass grows, and tomorrow will be mowed. Today the sun is hot; ice cream is cold. Father scrubs rust from the charcoal grill, and small stomachs cramp with sudden hunger for food that is burnt and leaks catsup.

Where I grew up, a parade still precedes darkness into town. It is led by the flag aloft, paced by drums and the proud, sour notes of young buglers. Kids in costume pass in review: George Washington, bewigged in cotton batting; clowns dour with embarrassment; a terrible cardboard dragon; Betsy Ross on a bicycle. Bands tune up by towering bonfires. Children run in circles as their elders dance in squares, and night slowly surrounds.

The very best is last—full dark, when the fireworks begin. The child in me stirs with suspense; I am ancient with nostalgia. Ever and ever it is the same—an intake of breath as the first rocket jets to heaven; the burst and spread of stars; the whole town saying, "Ahhh!"

Always at this moment I remember a night when, to my eye, the scene turned upside down. In the valley of the sky, the stars were as steady as streetlights; but earth's deep dark was populous with hurtling comets and meteors expiring in celestial sparks.

Always, too, as in my childhood, I feel a minor ache of melancholy when the life melts out of each starburst—but every next flight of rockets creates new stars. Aerial bombs wake echoes 12 months unheard. Pinwheels whirl dervishly, and Roman candles pop pink fireballs.

Light and noise fragment the sky; it is almost too much of much—and never quite enough. Even the grand finale fails to finish it. Children past their bedtime wave sparklers. "Look at me!" they cry, swirling traceries of white on the surface of the dark. "Look at *me*!"

I do look. I see the child I was, chasing the shadows of the children that are mine through summer days as fine and free as this one and summer nights sky-streaked with falling stars. Memory, the moment, the season's promise now are joined. Summer is in my heart and everywhere about.

Joan Mills

Now learn a parable of the fig tree; When his branch is yet tender, and putteth forth leaves, ye know that summer is nigh.

Matt. 24:32

GIVE ME THE SPLENDID SILENT SUN

*Give me the splendid silent sun with all
        its beams full-dazzling,
Give me juicy autumnal fruit ripe and red
        from the orchard,
Give me a field where the unmowed grass grows;
Give me an arbor, give me the trellised grape,
Give me fresh corn and wheat, give me serene-
        moving animals teaching content.
Give me nights perfectly quiet as on high
        plateaus west of the Mississippi, and
        I am looking up at the stars,
Give me odorous at sunrise a garden of
        beautiful flowers where I can walk
                undisturbed.*

Walt Whitman

THE HOMELAND

It's a certain voice, it's the sound
Of a bell in a distant tower,
It's sunlight on the ground
Through trees or after a shower,
It's a certain roof under a certain sky,
The fragrance of the path of a certain street,
A steeple with a farm kneeling near by,
The feeling of the grass under the feet,
The flash of a look, the faltering of a hand,
A something from the past, too quick to understand—
It's what one feels and cannot say
Even when one sings,
Though that's the nearest way,
It's all those things.

It's what one tastes and sees,
It's what one breathes and hears,
Tobacco, bread and cheese,
Bright leaves, a wind that veers,
The common sights and sounds,
Dogs barking, people greeting,
A mug of ale that pounds and pounds
A table at some meeting—
It's what one feels and cannot say
Even when one sings,
Though that's the nearest way,
It's all those things.

It's the body's very best,
It's the heartbeat in the side
For children at the breast,
It's remembering those who died,
It's the ardor of the way,
It's the savor of the song,
It's the dream, aching to stay,
And the passion, to belong,
The sower's will to reap,
The lover's will to keep—
It's what one feels and cannot say
Even when one sings—
Though that's the nearest way,
It's all these things.

by Émile Cammaerts
translated by Witter Bynner

Freedom is like the sap running in a tree. It sends
forth buds that blossom and bear fruit, when the time is ripe.

Hebe Weenolsen

BARTER

Life has loveliness to sell,
    All beautiful and splendid things,
Blue waves whitened on a cliff,
    Soaring fire that sways and sings,
And children's faces looking up
Holding wonder like a cup.

Life has loveliness to sell,
    Music like a curve of gold,
Scent of pine trees in the rain,
    Eyes that love you, arms that hold,
And for your spirit's still delight,
Holy thoughts that star the night.

Spend all you have for loveliness,
    Buy it and never count the cost;
For one white singing hour of peace
    Count many a year of strife well lost,
And for a breath of ecstasy
Give all you have been, or could be.

Sara Teasdale

TWO SUMMERS I HAVE KNOWN

When I was very young I wrote a poem called "Summer's End," which tried to describe the loss I felt at the close of what had been a special summer. And although being grown up means, I suppose, being able to open your hands and let things go, there's a part of me that wants to hold them fast.

Yes, I want to hold them fast, and one of the ways to keep them is to keep them alive inside my heart and my head. There, clearer and more real to me than photographs in an album, are the pictures of special summers in my life.

Pretty Summer

Somewhere around sixth grade I came to harbor the dread suspicion that I positively was not a good-looking girl. By seventh grade my suspicions were cruelly confirmed. In eighth grade the glorious Patty Norton— how I remember her!—stood for all the beauty in this world, and for her long dark hair and turned-up nose and violet eyes I very gladly would have sold my soul. In ninth grade and in tenth I was in love with Herman, who told my friends he found me homely but nice, and who kissed me a couple of times (which made me his forevermore) before going off with beautiful Eileen. I mean it when I say that I've never recovered.

I think of myself, in those four long years, deciding that love would never be given to me, that in spite of my mother's insincere "It's what's inside that counts," love was for the Pattys and Eileens. Because . . . they were pretty.

And then one special summer—I was 15½—a miracle happened: My homeliness went away, with a suddenness akin to being tapped with a golden wand by a fairy godmother. My shape, my skin, my face, my hair, even the failed orthodontia on my teeth, no longer conspired to make me a homely girl. Reflected in the mirror—and that summer I was looking in plenty of mirrors—was a brand-new me.

Now, I don't for a minute mean to suggest that I turned into a teen-aged Candy Bergen. I was never a raving beauty, but—good enough. On a blanket of pretty girls at the New Jersey seashore that sweet August, I now was another one of the pretty girls, instead of the homely girl that some people called "nice."

And one unforgettable day that summer as I stood all alone on the beach, gazing dreamily out at the ocean, a boy walked up behind me, took me by my shoulders and slowly . . . slowly . . . slowly turned me around. "I wanted to see if you looked as good from the front as you do from the back," is what he told me. Then . . . he paused for a perfect moment and said, "You do."

Family Summer

My youngest son was born in March, and by mid-July, I had a terminal case of Domestic Despair, for I felt myself to be pudgy, nasty, boring, overwhelmed and—I was right.

With a diaper-rashed infant and two other children under the age of six and no outside help (the woman who helped me was ill), I seemed to be folding laundry day and night. And eating too much. And snarling too much. And far too easily bursting into tears. And drowning my husband in conversations like, "Tony kicked Nick again." And, "Butter's gone up." And, "I can't seem to find a detergent to get these socks white."

That whole summer long I had this painful sense

that I'd lost myself, that I'd turned into someone I'd never intended to be, that my sweetness had curdled, my brain had gone soft and that even my laughter had somehow abandoned me.

I was in this grim mood when we all went away to Cape Cod for a couple of weeks, taking along the changer, the crib and the bikes, and taking, too, a list of noble goals I hoped to achieve by the end of the summer:

1. Lose eight pounds.

2. Do not discuss detergents with Milton at dinner. Discuss *War and Peace.* Or the Common Market. Or whether it is possible for a free society to tolerate any form of censorship or whether, on the other hand . . .

3. Do not swear at the children. Try to understand the needs and fears that underlie their rotten behavior.

4. Try to see the glass as half full, not half empty.

That summer Tony (still kicked Nick but he) learned to ride a two-wheeler. And our (still fiercely diaper-rashed) baby cooed at the waves. And our vital, inquisitive Nick (still getting in trouble every day) explored the wonders of sea life revealed at low tide. Meanwhile I lounged in my chair on the sand and I did start *War and Peace,* which I (sometimes) mentioned to Milton during dinner (along with the inadequacies of detergents plus the rising price of butter). And thanks to the swimming and walks on the beach (and in spite of the pizza, the French fries, the burgers, the shakes), I remained only eight pounds overweight that summer.

And sometime that summer I started to lose my case of Domestic Despair. And sometime that summer I seemed to recover my laughter. For somewhere along the way—though I still can't do it every day—I began to see that my glass was half full, not half empty.

Judith Viorst

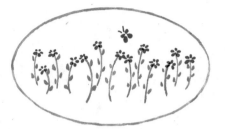

SUMMER'S RADIANCE

If we had never before looked upon the earth, but suddenly came to it man or woman grown, set down in the midst of a summer mead, would it not seem to us a radiant vision? The hues, the shapes, the song and life of birds, above all the sunlight, the breath of heaven, resting on it; the mind would be filled with its glory, unable to grasp it, hardly believing that such things could be mere matter and no more. Like a dream of some spirit-land it would appear, scarce fit to be touched lest it should fall to pieces, too beautiful to be long watched lest it should fade away. So it seemed to me as a boy, sweet and new like this each morning; and even now, after the years that have passed, and the lines they have worn in the forehead, the summer mead shines as bright and fresh as when my foot first touched the grass.

Richard Jefferies

Carefree summer days that stretched into warm, lazy evenings with family dinner picked fresh from the garden. These are some cherished memories of boyhood recalled by Philip B. Kunhardt, Jr.

On those heavy, humming August evenings we ate dinner on the screened porch. We would get the water racing in a big pot on the kitchen stove and then we would go up to our vegetable garden in a field behind the house and pick three dozen ear of corn—six apiece for my mother and for us and an even dozen for my father—and we would run them back to the kitchen so they wouldn't lose their sugar, do a quick shucking and toss them into the steaming pot. Making typewriters out of our teeth, we ate the corn slathered with butter and salt and pepper. My father took the little blade of his gold penknife and slit the rows down the middle so that the meat would pop out when he bit and the skin of each kernel wouldn't get caught in his teeth. As we ate, the sky lost its glow, orange slipping into black. A breeze out of the north made the trees shiver; leaves brushed against the screen like soft fingers. Over the razz of the katydids we talked in hushed voices, planning a swim before bed, deciding who would sleep with my father on the porch. We lugged mattresses off our beds, led them down the steep stairs like elephants and threw them trumpeting onto the porch floor. Then we stepped outside, took off any little clothing we might be wearing, made skirts of towels and headed down through the garden to the long, twisting, stony path that went to the pool. My father led the way, and blindfolded by night, we could just make out the white heap he made ahead of us.

GROWING TOGETHER

Last night, when I could not sleep, something in the wind rattling the glass of our bedroom windows, something in the faint stirrings of autumn that seeped the scents of turning foliage into the room, made me remember a night at the end of another summer about fifteen years ago.

The night I remembered was one at the beginning of autumn, a month or so after Dean was born, when Diana and I attended a farewell party for our neighbor's sons. The older boy was leaving for a year's study at a college in Europe and the younger one was departing for a job on a farm in the Middle West.

We spent several festive hours laughing and drinking. Toward the end of the evening, the two youths, singing and dancing a boisterous duet, their arms linked, their heads inclined against one another, re-created a performance they had apparently played many times before. Their father and mother watched them with an unmistakable sadness. . . .

Diana and I went home a short while later and long after we were in bed, in the darkness of our house, I lay awake listening to the sounds of revelry and music floating faintly across the night. . . .

In those last moments before I fell asleep, I recalled the sadness mingled with pride and love in the faces of my neighbors as they watched their sons. But with my own sons asleep and secure around me, sons too small for journeys of their own, I could not then comprehend that sadness because it was born of years and experiences I had not yet lived.

Five years, ten years . . . experiences flowing together. Birthdays and holidays, tryouts for school plays and school sports, disappointments and triumphs, clothing rapidly outgrown and endless piles of wash, first girlfriends and the deepening of voices, graduations and dilemmas, a driver's permit, the first son at the wheel of a car.

Often, in these years, I came to realize that however different they seemed from my own youth, under their irreverent and scoffing demeanors their longings and needs were about the same as ours had been . . . altered only by their own language and set to the indescribable rhythm of their music which had to be played at a deafening pitch. And after hours of discussion that continued late into the night, I would have an eerie sense of a ritual I had shared in before, words spoken between my father and myself many years ago. I came to understand, not without sadness, that they would seek their own experiences as I had sought my own, unable to accept my counsel in the same way I had been unable to accept the exhortations of my father.

Ten years . . . fifteen years . . . a passage of time bringing us where we stand now.

And our sons grown to young men, twenty-four, twenty and fourteen, the older boys bearded and mustached, shaggy apparitions appearing from time to time at our door, returning from sojourns in another city, from semesters at school, from summers overseas, hiking and wandering. Only Dean still lives with us at home.

At those rare moments now when we are all together, sitting around the table once again as we did when they were children, relishing their mother's food, they laugh, still argue, display spirits and minds of their own, sharing the stories and experiences and meanings they have discovered for themselves.

Now, in the heart of the night, the same stars glittering above me, but fifteen years added to my life, I understand what I could not fathom that night when our neighbors gave the farewell party for their sons: How almost all of life is made up of journeys, beginning with our own departures from our parents' houses, our leavetakings and homecomings, the decampments of our sons and daughters, the migration of birds over the track of forest and mountains, the swoopings of wind crossing and recrossing the land, all the recurring voyages and flights and partings carrying us toward that vast silence wherein we make the final, irrevocable journey each of us must travel alone.

For movement and change are the wellsprings of life, each age forced to recognize and accept anew the irredeemable truth that one generation passes, another generation rises, and the earth, the strange, enigmatic earth burned with the suns of fire and love, the earth endures. . . .

Harry Mark Petrakis

Every experience God gives us, every person He puts in our lives, is the perfect preparation for the future that only He can see.

Corrie Ten Boom

YOUR WORLD

Your world is as big as you make it.
I know, for I used to abide
In the narrowest nest in a corner,
My wings pressing close to my side.

But I sighted the distant horizon
Where the skyline encircled the sea
And I throbbed with a burning desire
To travel this immensity.

I battered the cordons around me
And cradled my wings on the breeze
Then soared to the uttermost reaches
With rapture, with power, with ease!

Georgia Douglas Johnson

MY SON LEAVES FOR SCHOOL

My son leaves for school
and he is less a boy
and more a man
every day.
I am seeing it happen
right before
my eyes
and accepting it.
Am I?
Then why must I remind him
of something
he almost forgot
on his way
out the door
and rejoice
when he seems
to still need me—
or does he?
And could he manage
through the day
without
that particular
book
or pencil
or me?
I think I know he could
for he is less
a boy
and more a man
every day.

Rae Turnbull

REFLECTIONS ON AUTUMN

What a time is autumn! It is filled with light and
color, with deep-blue skies, blazing stars, and in one part
of the world, with such a magnificence of gold and ruby,
scarlet and grape, yellow and bronze, that the heart
almost stops at the contemplation of it.

The tender uncertainty, the reluctant bloom, the
fresh renewal of spring have gone. Gone, too, are the
lush green ways of summer, the heavy heat, the brooding
storms, the lavish spilling forth of sunshine, of quiet rain,
and of flowers. In their place we have the mellow warm
days, the cool sweet nights. To drive through, or walk in,
the woods is unforgettable, or to sit out of doors and
watch the red moon rise and hear the wind come rushing
through the branches. As the days grow shorter they
become more measurable, and every minute is packed
with wonder and excitement. In autumn there is no time
to waste.

Each year that I live brings me closer to the
knowledge of the power and the glory. When you are
young, so much is taken for granted—the bird on the
wing, the flower in the grass, the sleepy song of brooks,
the changing skies. These and more—a friend's smile, the
touch of a beloved hand, children laughing at their play, a
dusty dog running home along a dusty road. The simple
things, and many that are not so simple. But when you
grow into maturity, into age, nothing can be taken for
granted. Each day must be lived completely and none
wasted. The brilliant leaf is one of millions, but each
holds the power and the glory, and must so be
contemplated.

Faith Baldwin

I HAVE ALWAYS SAID I WOULD GO

I have always said I would go sometime in the autumn
   Away from the bare boughs and the fallen leaves,
Away from the lonely sounds and the faded colors,
   And all the ancient sorrow, and change that grieves.

I have always said I would go—and now it's autumn—
   To an island where the wild hibiscus grows
And parakeets flock to the groves at twilight
   And fragrance drifts from bays where moonlight
      glows.

But there would be the vasty sound of breakers
   Come in to toss their pearls upon the sand.
All through the night—a longing of great waters
   Trying to make the vastness understand.

I have always said I would go sometime in the autumn
   Away from the lonely sounds and change that
      grieves—
But here in my heart is the sound of a distant ocean
   And here in my heart is the sound of these falling
      leaves.

Glenn Ward Dresbach

SEPTEMBER . . . A GENTLE MONTH

September is now fading into eternity, taking the last of this year's summer with it. It has been a gentle month, preparing us for the cold weather and the bareness that will soon settle over the garden. I am grateful for its many golden days and even for its rain, and as it departs, I feel like reaching out my hand, as to an old friend who must leave just when we have begun to enjoy each other's company.

In my heart I bless September and, bidding it good-by, I brace myself for the future months. Just like life, I think. We don't like to let go of the autumn years of our lives. Rather than face old age, we cling to those good years and we forget that our wonderful Creator has promised us a beautiful sunset in the garden of life if we love and trust Him with all our hearts. We must follow the pattern of life, year by year, but to us is given the fortitude to meet each new day.

Thyra Ferré Bjorn

Listen. . . .
With faint dry sound
Like steps of passing ghosts,
The leaves, frost-crisped, break from the trees
And fall.

Adelaide Crapsey

OCTOBER

It's a quiet, blessed month. I used to love the early spring the best, but now I'm in the fall of life and the fall of the year agrees with my advancing years. Everything is calm and mellow and ripe. . . . The walnut trees have faded and are dropping their fruit. Persimmons are ripe and possum too. The little boys are pulling their pop corn and digging their goobers and gathering chestnuts and haws and May pops. The nights are getting long and a little fire takes off the evening chill and cheers the family hearth-stone. Now is the time to read and write and have some old-time music.

Bill Arp

BROWN GOLD

The time of the brown gold comes softly.
Oat shocks are alive in brown gold belts,
*   the short and the shambling oat shocks*
*   sit on the stubble and straw.*
The timothy hay, the fodder corn, the cabbage
*   and the potatoes, across their leaves are*
*   footsteps.*
There is a bold green up over the cracks in
*   the corn rows where the crickets go criss-*
*   cross errands, where the bugs carry packages.*
Flutter and whirr, you birdies, you newcomers
*   in lines and sashes, tellers of harvest*
*   weather on the way, belts of brown gold*
*   coming softly.*
It is very well the old time streamers take
*   up the old time gold haze against the*
*   western timber line.*
It is the old time again when months and birds
*   tell each other, "Oh, very well," and repeat it*
*   where the fields and the timber lines meet*
*   in belts of brown gold hazes, "Oh, very*
*   well, Oh, very well."*

Carl Sandburg

A GRATEFUL PAUSE

"Every morning of the world I give thanks for all the wonderful things in my life," declared a young man enthusiastically. "And do you know something? It's strange indeed, but the more I give thanks, the more I have reason to be thankful. For, you see, blessings just pile up on me one after another like nobody's business."

This exultant expression interested me, for I well remembered this young fellow and the long way he had come in achieving this attitude. In his remarks he had stated a basic law: The more you practice the art of thankfulness, the more you have to be thankful for. This, of course, is a fact. Thankfulness does tend to reproduce in kind. It reverses the flow of life's good away from you and sets flowing in your direction benefits and opportunities. The attitude of gratitude revitalizes the entire mental process by activating all other attitudes, thus stimulating creativity. It focuses the whole personality so that you can work better, think better, get along better with people and, in short, use your abilities to function more effectively in every respect.

Norman Vincent Peale

O give thanks unto the Lord; call upon his name: make known his deeds among the people.

Ps. 105:1

THOUGHT FOR THANKSGIVING

A scarlet tulip nodding in the breeze.
The dewy freshness of an April morn.
A calf just born.
The endless vastness of the pounding sea.
The quiet peace of snow that falls at night.
The geese in flight.
The smell of earth fresh-turned beneath the plow.
A misty rainbow arching through the sky.
A butterfly.
The gentle whisper of cascading leaves.
A gang of puppies romping in the sun.
The day's work done.

We take Thy blessings, Lord, all through the year
Without a word of thanks until, today,
We pause to pray.

Barbara Parsons Hildreth

APPRECIATION

When Charles A. Lindbergh sighted the southern tip of Ireland at the close of his first trans-Atlantic flight he recorded: "One senses only through change, appreciates only after absence. I haven't been far enough away to know the earth before. For twenty-five years I've lived on it, and yet not seen it till this moment. For nearly two thousand hours, I've flown over it without realizing what wonders lay below, what crystal clarity—snow-white foam on black-rock shores—curving hill above its valley—the hospitality of little houses—the welcome of waving arms. During my entire life I've accepted these gifts of God to man, and not known what was mine until this moment. It's like rain after drought; spring after a northern winter. I've been to eternity and back."

The earth is the Lord's, and the fulness thereof; the world, and they that dwell therein.

Ps. 24:1

Give us, Lord, a bit o' sun
A bit o' work and a bit o' fun;
Give us all in the struggle and sputter
Our daily bread and a bit o' butter;
Give us health, our keep to make,
An' a bit to spare for others' sake.
Give us sense, for we're some of us duffers,
An' a heart to feel for all that suffers;
Give us, too, a bit of song
And a tale, and a book to help us along.
An' give us our share of sorrow's lesson
That we may prove how grief's a blessin'.
Give us, Lord, a chance to be
Our goodly best for ourselves and others
Till all men learn to live as brothers.

Inscribed on the wall of an old
inn in Lancaster, England

NOVEMBER SKIES

Than these November skies
Is no sky lovelier. The clouds are deep;
Into their grey the subtle spies
Of colour creep,
Changing that high austerity to delight,
Till even the leaden interfolds are bright.
And, where the cloud breaks, faint far azure peers
Ere a thin flushing cloud again
Shuts up that loveliness, or shares.
The huge great clouds move slowly, gently, as
Reluctant the quick sun should shine in vain,
Holding in bright caprice their rain.
*   And when of colours none,*
Nor rose, nor amber, nor the scarce late green
Is truly seen,—
In all the myriad grey,
In silver height and dusky deep, remain
The loveliest,
Faint purple flushes of the unvanquished sun.

John Freeman

Winter brings a quiet time for growing things to rest. The mystery of nature is most evident to me as seeds sleep beneath the full tide of snow and sap is quiescent in the maples. Now we know the snow itself nourishes the earth, bringing nitrogen. Only the evergreens seem unchanged, except the green is darker. Or is it because of the white world around?

Gladys Taber

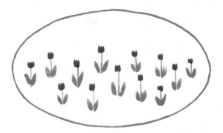

One kind word can warm three winter months.

Japanese Proverb

VELVET SHOES

Let us walk in the white snow
    In a soundless space;
With footsteps quiet and slow,
    At a tranquil pace,
Under veils of white lace.

I shall go shod in silk,
    And you in wool,
White as a white cow's milk,
    More beautiful
Than the breast of a gull.

We shall walk through the still town
    In a windless peace;
We shall step upon the white down,
    Upon silver fleece,
Upon softer than these.

We shall walk in velvet shoes:
    Wherever we go
Silence will fall like dews
    On white silence below.
We shall walk in the snow.

Elinor Wylie

THE DARK DAYS OF WINTER—A TIME OF
WAITING AND BELIEVING . . .

As far back as the race memories run, the winter solstice has been a time of questioning and wonder that led to rediscovery of the basic certainties. It wasn't by chance that it became the occasion for religious events that we now speak of, in our offhand way, as The Holidays. It was, and still is, a holy time in the deepest sense. When we see the sun stand still, far off toward the south, and then swing north, lengthening the daylight after steady weeks of abbreviation, we are witness to a cosmic miracle.

It doesn't really matter that we now explain it in terms of celestial order and rhythm, with their inevitable consequences. Rationalize it as we may, there is some force behind it; and all our intricate calculations can do is state the How and the Why in terms of elaborate equations. They can't get at the What, which lies beyond, the inevitability itself. We have to take that on faith.

A wise old countryman once said to me, "Every winter I have to renew my belief." And when I asked, "Belief in what?" he said, "My belief in believing."

That is the gist of it, stated with the utmost economy. Belief is easy in June, with summer all around you. In fact, doubt is difficult in a green and hospitable world. The test comes in December, when you have to believe that onsetting winter will pass. You have to muster the deep-down belief that hope is not foolish and faith is not futile. You have to believe in your own believing.

Hal Borland

STOPPING BY WOODS ON A SNOWY EVENING

Whose woods these are I think I know.
His house is in the village, though;
He will not see me stopping here
To watch his woods fill up with snow.

My little horse must think it queer
To stop without a farmhouse near
Between the woods and frozen lake
The darkest evening of the year.

He gives his harness bells a shake
To ask if there is some mistake.
The only other sound's the sweep
Of easy wind and downy flake.

The woods are lovely, dark, and deep,
But I have promises to keep,
And miles to go before I sleep,
And miles to go before I sleep.

Robert Frost

Other holidays honor one to four of the senses, but Christmas honors all five senses: taste with its special foods; and touch with fire and warmth; and hearing with music; and sight with trees and tinsel. More than any other holiday, it also respects the sense of smell. Among the three gifts brought to Bethlehem by the Wise Men, the Scriptures tell us, two—frankincense and myrrh—appealed to the sense of smell. So Christmas should be remembered for the scents of pine, oranges, ginger, and cloves.

Eugene McCarthy

And the angel said unto them, Fear not: for, behold, I
bring you good tidings of great joy, which shall be to all
people.
For unto you is born this day in the city of David a
Saviour, which is Christ the Lord.

Luke 2:10,11

The raw materials of the Christmas mood are a
newborn baby, a family, friendly animals, and labor. An
endless process of births is the perpetual answer of life to
the fact of death. It says that life keeps coming on, keeps
seeking to fulfill itself, keeps affirming the margin of hope
in the presence of desolation, pestilence and despair.

Howard Thurman

HEAVENLY CHILD

The world is at peace, but war has left its victims, none more pitiable than the children of Vietnam, to whom many Americans have opened their hearts and their homes.

The tiny parking lot behind the Happy Hours Kindergarten was already filled but they found a space across the street. Even from there, they could hear the children singing carols loudly.

"Well, it's noisier than it was in September," Molly said, trying to laugh. "Remember how sort of strained it was then, meeting all those parents and children for the first time? And Kim so quiet. . . ."

"She sure wasn't quiet tonight," Louis said, as they got out of the car. "The whole time I was driving her over she never stopped chattering about the picture she's going to show us and the fact that she got picked to come early to help mix the punch. She's made a great adjustment, honey. Don't forget, these are the first children she's really had a chance to know."

"And the first complete families," Molly added, "ones she could relate to." Their own friends were mostly the parents of teen-agers. She and Lou had waited a long time before they accepted the fact that there would be no child of their own, longer still before they had seriously considered adoption.

When they had finally made the decision, however, they had been in complete accord about the next step. Their parents and friends had been startled. Even now, five years later, Molly could recall her mother's concern: "But *why* a Vietnamese baby? Surely you can qualify for a child from a local agency, one of your own race. . . ."

"Children like that are more easily placed," Molly had explained. "Lou and I want to share our lives with a child who needs us, a child who wouldn't have a home if we didn't take him."

"You're asking for problems," her mother had said worriedly. "Granted, there is nothing cuter than an Oriental baby, but when he gets older and compares his family to others, will he ever really feel he belongs?"

"Of course," Molly had cried, thrusting the warning from her.

But had she, she now wondered, disposed of it too quickly? Would it come back to haunt her on this peaceful night of the children's party?

Kim had defied them right from the start by not being "a cute Oriental baby." The child who was carried out to them at the airport was pathetic. Dull eyes stared lifelessly out from under a tangle of dirty hair; a distended belly bulged beneath a cheap cotton dress. Matchstick arms hung limply.

When Molly had reached out, Kim had begun to cry.

"She's frightened," the woman from the agency had said. "She's had a hard time. You'll win her over. Just feed her and love her."

"We will," Molly had promised.

And they *had* fed her and loved her. Oh, how they had loved her! And how wonderful it had been to watch her become a truly heavenly child, robust and happy.

Kim was over two years old when she finally began to walk and, at about the same time, she began to speak.

Her first words were "Mama" and "Dada," to her parents' delight, and Molly's mother, whose heart had been won completely, had started a campaign to teach her to say "Nana."

By the time she was four, Kim had become a definite personality, funny, endearing and stubborn. She had also developed a strong feeling about her own identity.

"I am Kim Jordan," she would say in a tone that invited no argument. "My daddy is Louis Jordan. My mommy is Molly Jordan. My grandma is Nana Jordan."

"No. Grandma is Nana Elliot," Molly would correct her. "She has a different name from ours."

But Kim would not accept this. "No," she would state firmly. "We are all in one family, all the same."

"I guess it's time we went into the adoption story with her," Lou said when he heard this.

So that night they had sat on Kim's bed and told her about their loneliness before she came to them, and about how they had sent away to a far country. . . .

"What was I doing there?" Kim asked. "In that funny place all by myself?"

"You were born there," Louis began.

Kim interrupted. "That's a dumb story. Tell something good."

So Louis had told *Goldilocks* and, listening, Molly had become fully conscious for the first time how much little brown bears looked like big brown bears, and how vulnerable her child was.

She mustn't be hurt, Molly had thought fiercely. She mustn't ever be hurt.

And at the same time the question had risen unbidden within her: Did we do the right thing? Will she thank us later? Or will the time come when she looks at us and sees us not as parents but as members of an alien race with white skin and round eyes?

The thought had come even stronger when it was time to start Kim in kindergarten. It was Louis who brought up Happy Hours.

"It's got a good reputation," he said. "It's fully integrated, with a little of everything. A Japanese guy at work sends his boy there."

"These other kids," Molly had asked, "are they . . . from mixed families like ours?"

"Who knows?" Louis had said. "They're having an open house next Thursday. We can go and find out what it's all about."

So they had enrolled Kim. Molly had known in her heart that this was best. They had attended the open house and the families had been there—white, black, red, and golden-skinned families—but each consistent within itself.

Kim had clung to Molly's hand. She had stared about her silently through widened eyes, and Molly had thought: She sees. She is beginning to realize. It will not be long.

That had been in the fall. As the next months passed, Kim's initial shyness vanished. She liked her teachers. She liked painting. She liked music and games and making letters.

"But she seems different," Molly remarked to Louis. "We're not as close. It's as though she's turning outward, toward other people, away from us."

"Isn't that natural?" Louis had answered. "After all, she's not a baby. It's time she became more independent. Don't worry so, honey. Kim loves us; she knows we love her."

And now he said the same thing.

As they crossed the snowy lawn the noise grew louder, and when they went in it poured upon them in a wave of festivity. The big front room was ablaze with color; paper streamers of red and green draped the ceiling, and a tall tree glowed with rainbow lights. In the center a long table held platters of cookies and a shimmering punch bowl.

People were everywhere—mothers, fathers, grandparents— but the kindergartners themselves were the stars. They rushed about, chirping like happy sparrows, as they dragged adults by the hand, pointing out paintings and projects, giggling and squealing and bubbling with joy.

Kim was standing motionless beside the punch bowl. When she saw Louis and Molly her face came to life. Handing the ladle to the girl beside her, she worked her way toward them. "Did you see my picture?" she asked.

"Not yet," Molly said. "Where is it?"

"There on the wall," Kim said.

Turning, Molly saw that the far wall was covered with children's drawings. Two dozen proud Josephs guarded two dozen gentle Marys, and two dozen mangers tilted precariously in as many directions. Angels perched daringly on rooftops, and a varied assortment of lopsided stars gleamed on high.

"Which is yours?" Molly asked, and even as she spoke she felt her husband's arm go around her. His other hand dropped to rest on his daughter's glossy black head.

Then she saw it—the picture of the blond Joseph bent protectively over his blonde Mary. From the manger, on a mound of hay so high that any less perfect babe would have rolled off onto the stable floor, a raven-haired, almond-eyed Baby beamed contentedly up at His parents.

Lois Duncan

The wolf also shall dwell with the lamb, and the leopard
shall lie down with the kid; and the calf and the young
lion and the fatling together; and a little child shall lead
them.
And the cow and the bear shall feed; their young ones
shall lie down together: and the lion shall eat straw like
the ox.
And the sucking child shall play on the hole of the asp,
and the weaned child shall put his hand on the cockatrice'
den.
They shall not hurt nor destroy in all my holy mountain:
for the earth shall be full of the knowledge of the Lord, as
the waters cover the sea.

Isa. 11:6-9

One day, Count Leo Tolstoy was stopped by a beggar who seemed weak, emaciated, and starving. The author searched his pockets for a coin but discovered that he was without a single penny. Taking the beggar's worn hands between his own, he said: "Do not be angry with me, my brother; I have nothing with me." The lined face of the beggar became illumined as he replied: "But you called me brother—that was a great gift."

James C. Humes

I have a dream today . . .

I have a dream that one day every valley shall be exalted, every hill and mountain shall be made low, the rough places will be made plain, and the crooked places will be made straight. And the glory of the Lord shall be revealed, and all flesh shall see it together.

This is our hope. This is the faith with which I return to the South. With this faith we will be able to hew out of the mountain of despair a stone of hope. With this faith we will be able to transform the jangling discords of our nation into a beautiful symphony of brotherhood. With this faith we will be able to work together . . . to stand up for freedom together, knowing that we will be free one day.

Martin Luther King, Jr.

From where I'm sitting, tolerance is just a big word for peace. War can't get going where there's a sympathetic understanding of nation for nation, man for man, and creed for creed.

Bing Crosby

THOMAS JEFFERSON'S RULES OF LIVING

Never put off till tomorrow what you can do today.
Never trouble another for what you can do yourself.
Never spend your money before you have it.
Never buy what you do not want because it is cheap.
Pride costs us more than hunger, thirst, and cold.
We seldom repent having eaten too little.
Nothing is troublesome that we do willingly.
How much pain the evils have cost us that have never
    happened!
Take things always by the smooth handle.
When angry, count ten before you speak: if very angry, a
    hundred.

A SMILE

A smile costs nothing, but gives much. It enriches those who receive, without making poorer those who give. It takes but a moment, but the memory of it sometimes lasts forever. None is so rich or mighty that he can get along without it, and none is so poor but that he can be made rich by it. A smile creates happiness in the home, fosters good will in business, and is the countersign of friendship. It brings rest to the weary, cheer to the discouraged, sunshine to the sad, and it is nature's best antidote for trouble. Yet it cannot be bought, begged, borrowed, or stolen, for it is something that is of no value to anyone until it is given away. Some people are too tired to give you a smile. Give them one of yours, as none needs a smile so much as he who has no more to give.

Author Unknown

I think we all admire people who live generously, with open hearts and hands. I envy them. I have a feeling that a good many of us, certainly including myself, conduct our lives rather as banks do business, open at certain hours only, on certain days of the week.

Bentz Plagemann

ACCOMPLISHMENT

If you have known how to compose your life, you have accomplished a great deal more than the man who knows how to compose a book. Have you been able to take your stride? You have done more than the man who has taken cities and empires.

The great and glorious masterpiece of man is to live to the point. All other things—to reign, to hoard, to build—are, at most, but inconsiderate props and appendages.

The truly wise man must be as intelligent and expert in the use of natural pleasures as in all the other functions of life. So the sages live, gently yielding to the laws of our human lot, to Venus and to Bacchus. Relaxation and versatility, it seems to me, go best with a strong and noble mind, and do it singular honor. There is nothing more notable in Socrates than that he found time, when he was an old man, to learn music and dancing, and thought it time well spent.

Montaigne

I said, Days should speak, and multitude of years should teach wisdom.

Job 32:7

COME HOME

What is this strange compulsion to go home again? The place you were so anxious to leave, yet can never leave altogether. Too much of you is rooted there. You thought that you were tearing yourself free, bloodily by the roots, yet fragments always remain tenaciously. They are stronger than you think. They tug at you when you go back, they tease and torment you. They people the street with ghosts, one of them yourself. "This is where you began, where you belong. Come back!" they seem to call.

Yet as Thomas Wolfe said, "You can't go home again." The change is almost too much to bear. And yet the sameness, the sweet tantalizing sameness . . .

When I was home the spring before Mother died we all piled into the car one night after supper and went for a ride. It was sunset, one of those dazzling, burning sunsets that turn the lake to molten gold and stirred me so as a girl. The same docks jutted, the same gulls wheeled, the same droves of little black mudhens were riding, plunging, riding their crests as the same tireless waves foamed in. The lake, mysterious old gray-green friend, was rolling in as it has for generations. Grandpa Griffith was chased across it by the wolves one winter. Grandpa and Grandma fished here, Mother and Dad courted in its shady parks. And so did we. Every walk and bench and statue is a silent shout of memories.

Laughter, a merry uniting of memories along with that dull ache . . . Our pilgrimage draws us ever farther into the past. There stands the house where my brother was born. There the house where my parents were married. There even the small white cottage behind a hedge "where Dad and I met," Mother says. "At a church party. I'd come with another boy, but he walked me home."

Incredible! It mustn't be there any more in its prim white dignity, looking as it must have looked that night. For now, impossibly, one parent is gone and the other is old and must soon be going. "Come back!" the mute houses are crying. "Nothing is different, nothing is changed. Come home." . . .

A few months later the phone rang: it was the call I'd been expecting, and it said, "Come home."

A hometown puts its arms around you when a parent dies. It gathers you to itself like a child. It feeds and comforts you. People surround you, warm living people, and they too say with their food and flowers and their eyes: "Stay. Oh, don't go away again, stay home."

But it was Dick, a boy I grew up with, who put it into words after the sermon: "Come back, Marj. We need you. This is where you belong."

I felt strangled. There had been nothing for me here in years; why now? Why this strange compulsion now? For the temptation, however absurd, was intense, and the rejection violent.

"You don't understand. I couldn't." . . .

We spent days breaking up her home. Boxing up memories, keepsakes, and photographs that we'd probably never look at again but couldn't bear to part with. Dividing things, giving things away, cleaning. I walked across the backyard to throw out some trash. The arbor needed painting but still supported the torrent of red roses Dad had set out years ago and took such pride in. They climbed all over the garage and trailed the ground, greedy with life. They were almost too fragrant in the hot sun, their petals spilling. Great trees still arched the yard as if still waiting for family picnics on the grass, great gatherings of the clan. Mother's bag of clothespins was still hanging on the line.

My sister came out and we maundered about the place, remembering. And I said, "Why is man the only creature to experience this awful tie with his past? Memory is both a blessing and a curse, it hurts to recall the days which are over."

"That's because we remember only the good things about them. Looking back it always seems so much better." Then she said, "But man needs memory. Without memory there wouldn't be any painters or writers—no doctors to help us, no engineers, no architects. Memory is what enables man to survive and progress."

And this is true, but it's more than that. Man is the only creature whose emotions are entangled with his memory. And the anguish of memory is what we probably must pay for its pleasures, or whatever progress we gain from it. Bitter or sweet, we don't want any part of life to be really over; it should always be available, if only through people who have shared it. When they go they take a part of you with them.

But the roots remain. The roots that will forever keep calling you back, begging, *"Come home!"*

Marjorie Holmes

One thing is certain as we grow older: The few people who have truly passed through us and we through them until the dreams, images, memories are past sorting out—these people become precious links to our continuity. That includes our parents, our children, our loves. If we try to bury the images of others who meant so much, part of us dies with them. How much greater our aliveness if we can come to a freestanding friendship with those who have shared us.

Gail Sheehy

Finish every day and be done with it. You have done what you could. Some blunders and absurdities no doubt crept in; forget them as soon as you can. Tomorrow is a new day; begin it well and serenely and with too high a spirit to be cumbered with your old nonsense. This day is all that is good and fair. It is too dear, with its hopes and invitations, to waste a moment on the yesterdays.

Ralph Waldo Emerson

This is the secret of joy. We shall no longer strive for our own way; but commit ourselves, easily and simply, to God's way, acquiesce in his will and in so doing find our peace.

Evelyn Underhill

HOW I WANT TO LIVE

I know how I want to live. I know what's good for me. I know what brings me joy. I know what has value and what doesn't. That doesn't mean that there aren't some nights when life seems bleak and I cry myself to sleep. Okay, all right, I'll say to myself, I'll give them tonight, but tomorrow is mine. Life has to be up and down—if it isn't down once in a while, how would I know what up is? So I don't pretend. When I'm miserable, I'm miserable, and I tell everybody I come in contact with. I never try to put on a happy face. I deal with it. I try to understand why. I fight my way out of it. And when I'm happy everybody knows about that too. So many people stop themselves from feeling good—that's so hard for me to understand. They can't even accept a compliment. God, when I feel good I do pirouettes!

Doris Day

For all the blessings life has brought,
For all its sorrowing hours have taught,
For all we mourn, for all we keep,
The hands we clasp, the loved that sleep,
We thank Thee, Father: let Thy grace
Our loving circle still embrace,
Thy mercy shed its heavenly store,
Thy peace be with us evermore.

Oliver Wendell Holmes

Happiness consists of sharing joy with others. Consider the fragrance of a delightful perfume. It cannot be experienced until the bottle is unsealed. So it is with happiness. Kept to itself, happiness is there but no one can enjoy it.

Edward L. Friedman

LET WAR'S TEMPESTS CEASE

Lord, let war's tempests cease,
Fold the whole world in peace
Under Thy wings.
Make all the nations one,
All hearts beneath the sun,
Till Thou shalt reign alone,
Great King of Kings.

Henry Wadsworth Longfellow

When the poet Henry Wadsworth Longfellow was well along in years his hair was white as snow, but his cheeks were as red as a rose. An admirer asked him how he was able to keep so vigorous and yet have time to write so beautifully. Pointing to a blossoming apple tree, the poet said, "That tree is very old, but I never saw prettier blossoms on it than those which it now bears. That tree grows new wood each year. Like that apple tree, I try to grow a little new wood each year."

James C. Humes

HOW OLD ARE YOU?

Age is a quality of mind.
If you have left your dreams behind,
If hope is cold,
If you no longer look ahead,
If your ambitions' fires are dead—
Then you are old.
But if from life you take the best,
If in life you keep the jest,
If love you hold;
No matter how the years go by,
No matter how the birthdays fly—
You are not old.

H. S. Fritsch

There are many ways to be tired, but some people never realize the difference. When you are physically and mentally tired in a negative way, that is a warning. You should rest. When you are beautifully tired, you should admit it and be thankful for the feeling. It comes when you've had a sense of accomplishment, hard work that paid off in satisfaction. When a man is beautifully tired and knows only that he is weary, he is making his own sadness. When happiness comes, he doesn't know it, but habitually calls it something else.

Pearl Bailey

JOY

And joy is everywhere; it is in the earth's green covering of grass; in the blue serenity of the sky; in the reckless exuberance of spring; in the severe abstinence of grey winter; in the living flesh that animates our bodily frame; in the perfect poise of the human figure, noble and upright; in living; in the exercise of all our powers; in the acquisition of knowledge; in fighting evils; in dying for gains we never can share. Joy is there everywhere; it is superfluous, unnecessary; nay, it very often contradicts the most peremptory behests of necessity. It exists to show that the bonds of law can only be explained by love; they are like body and soul. Joy is the realisation of the truth of oneness, the oneness of our soul with the world and of the world-soul with the supreme lover.

Rabindranath Tagore

A PRAYER

Let me do my work each day: and if the darkened hours of despair overcome me, may I not forget the strength that comforted me in the desolation of other times.

May I still remember the bright hours that found me walking over the silent hills of my childhood, or dreaming, on the margin of the quiet river, when a light glowed within me, and I promised my early God to have courage amid the tempests of the changing years. Spare me from bitterness and from the sharp passions of unguarded moments. May I not forget that poverty and riches are of the spirit. Though the world know me not, may my thoughts and actions be such as shall keep me friendly with myself.

Lift my eyes from the earth, and let me not forget the uses of the stars. Forbid that I should judge others lest I condemn myself. Let me not follow the clamor of the world, but walk calmly in my path.

Give me a few friends who will love me for what I am; and keep ever burning before my vagrant steps the kindly light of hope. And though age and infirmity overtake me, and I come not within sight of the castle of my dreams, teach me still to be thankful for life, and for time's olden memories that are good and sweet; and may the evening's twilight find me gentle still.

Max Ehrmann

ACKNOWLEDGMENTS

The editor and the publisher have made every effort to trace the ownership of all copyrighted material and to secure permission from copyright holders of such material. In the event of any question arising as to the use of any material the publisher and editor, while expressing regret for inadvertent error, will be pleased to make the necessary corrections in future printings. Thanks are due to the following authors, publishers, publications and agents for permission to use the material indicated.

THE ASSOCIATED PRESS, for "Dear Mom" by Hal Boyle as published in New York *World-Telegram And Sun* (May 12, 1956).

BARBARA DODGE BORLAND, for an excerpt from *Homeland* by Hal Borland. Copyright © 1964, 1965, 1966, 1967, 1968, 1969 by Hal Borland.

JAMES BROWN ASSOCIATES, INC. and NOEL R. PEATTIE, for "February Nineteenth" from *An Almanac For Moderns* by Donald Culross Peattie. Copyright © 1935 by Donald Culross Peattie.

THE WITTER BYNNER FOUNDATION FOR POETRY, INC., for "The Home-Land" by Emile Cammaerts from *A Canticle Of Pan*. Copyright © 1920 by Alfred P. Knopf, copyright © renewed 1948 by Witter Bynner.

THE CAXTON PRINTERS, LTD., for "I Have Always Said I Would Go" from *Collected Poems 1914-1948* by Glenn Ward Dresbach. Copyright © 1950 by the Caxton Printers, Ltd.

JOAN DAVES, for an excerpt from "I Have A Dream" by Martin Luther King, Jr. Copyright © 1963 by Martin Luther King, Jr.

JEAN REYNOLDS DAVIS, for "Let Me Grow" from *To God With Love* by Jean Reynolds Davis. Published by Harper & Row, Publishers, Inc. Copyright © 1968 by Jean Reynolds Davis.

DOUBLEDAY & COMPANY, INC., for "A Mellow Month" by Bill Arp from *Day By Day With Celestine Sibley* by Celestine Sibley. Copyright © 1975 by Celestine Sibley; for an excerpt from *Anne Frank: The Diary Of A Young Girl* by Anne Frank. Copyright © 1952 by Otto H. Frank. British Commonwealth rights granted by Vallentine, Mitchell & Co., Ltd., London; for "How Old Are You?" by H.S. Fritsch from *Poems That Live Forever* selected by Hazel Felleman. Copyright © 1965 by Doubleday & Company, Inc.; for an excerpt from *Adventures In Contentment* by David Grayson. Copyright © 1907 by Doubleday & Company, Inc.; for an excerpt from *The Last Englishman* by Hebe Weenolsen. Copyright © 1951 by Hebe Weenolsen.